7. 8- 03

INFANTRY PADRE

Infantry Padre

Revd. A.E. Gibbins
T.D., H.C.F.

Men that have hazarded their lives
for the name of our Lord Jesus Christ

Acts 15[26]

Pentland Books
Durham · Edinburgh · Oxford

© Revd. A.E. Gibbins 2001

First published in 2001 by
Pentland Books
1 Hutton Close
South Church
Bishop Auckland
Durham

British Library Cataloguing in Publication Data.
A catalogue record for this book is available
from the British Library.

ISBN 1 85821 852 7

Typeset by George Wishart & Associates, Whitley Bay.
Printed and bound by Antony Rowe Ltd., Chippenham.

*In memory of my wife, Margery,
without whose love and faith this
manuscript would not have survived.
And members of the 5th Btl. DCLI,
who hazarded their lives.*

Contents

List of Illustrations

Author's Note

In 1945 the Revd. Frank Cumbers asked me to write up the account of my service in Normandy as a Methodist Chaplain with the Duke of Cornwall's Light Infantry as fortunately I had survived and served with them throughout the whole campaign from June '44 to May '45 and said, 'I like the title'.

I accordingly wrote this up and finished it in India, where I had been posted, actually about to invade Malaya. Fortunately the Atom Bomb was ~~not~~ dropped and thousands of lives were saved including mine.

I sent the manuscript home to my wife to be typed and sent it to the War Office for permission to publish, which as a serving officer I was required to do so. Permission was refused and I forgot all about it.

My wife died on October 4th last year and on clearing up her affairs I discovered the original manuscript which I had retyped, and much to my surprise, a number of friends whose opinions I respect want it to reach a wider audience.

Foreword

by Sir David Willcocks, CBE, MC

Chaplains to the Forces have always had an important role to play, not least in ministering to those engaged in battle on the ground, at sea, or in the air. Their status as non-combatants has meant that many chaplains have not received the full recognition due to them for their service, despite the fact that they have shared the danger, mental and physical stress and discomfort of warfare. Through their personal courage and a strong sense of duty, doubtless derived in part at least from their religious faith, many chaplains have helped to boost the morale of those in their unit.

I am very pleased that the Reverend Albert Gibbins, who served as Padre of the 5th Battalion, The Duke of Cornwall's Light Infantry, from 1943-45 has written a short account of his experiences as Chaplain of an infantry battalion in the 43rd Wessex Division, which was engaged in many battles in Normandy, Holland and Germany between June 1944 and May 1945.

I shall always remember the dignity with which he conducted simple funeral services for the dead, both of our own and of enemy soldiers; the compassion he showed to the wounded; and his concern for all members of the battalion, regardless of denomination.'

There have been many books written by wartime commanders of fighting units, but I have not read any which describe in any detail the experiences of an army chaplain in the front line.

David Willcocks, Intelligence Officer
5th Battalion, The Duke of Cornwall's Light Infantry
(1941-1945)

Introduction

This is an account of a campaign as seen by a Padre. It makes no pretence at being an official record, but is written as a tribute to the men of the battalion with which I was privileged to serve, many of whom gave their all that we might live. I hope that this simple story will help in some measure to ensure that their sacrifice is not in vain, and that those of us who are returning may be met with sympathy and understanding as we seek to readjust ourselves to civilian life and especially in our relationship with Home and Church.

The story was started in Germany and finished in India and it has been difficult to achieve continuity owing to the author constantly moving and having to try and fish up the threads of his thoughts as and when possible. I hope therefore that faults of style and language may be forgiven.

Revd. A.E. Gibbins,   *India Command*
T.D., H.C.F.   *31 October, 1945*

Europe 1944. 43rd Division Chaplains.
Author is third from left back row.

Chapter One

I was posted to 214 Infantry Brigade in September 1943. Being a Methodist, the Brigadier immediately decided to attach me to the 5th Cornwall Light Infantry and so I found myself almost the sole North Countryman in an essentially West Country unit. Fortunately for me I had done a short spell of service in the west before joining the army and so was able to understand their language a little. Whether they understood mine or not was a different matter.

The Brigade had just finished a combined operation course and everyone was disappointed because the job for which they had trained was now cancelled. We were to cease being an independent Brigade and join the 43rd Division, and in October 1943 we arrived at the other end of England, in Sussex, faced with the task of settling into the Division and training hard. I discovered that the transport establishment for the padre was a motor-cycle and spent more than one nerve-racking afternoon in the Sussex lanes learning to balance this devil's invention on two wheels.

We were not left long in Sussex however, before the whole Division moved over into Kent and we discovered to our joy that our new home was to be Folkestone. True, it was a much battered Folkestone, but still a town, and better still, our billets were on the front in the best hotels – this was the life! We arrived at the beginning of November at about 3 o'clock in the afternoon and fortune smiled on us. The sun was shining, visibility was perfect and there across the Channel was the coast of France. The outpost of the Nazi Empire was in sight. How often afterwards we sat in the mess and looked at those same cliffs and wondered at the future.

In these surroundings we spent the winter, which involved much hard training, and big 'schemes' in the Stone Street area – how we learnt to hate that particular bit of Kent – but always the return to comparative comfort in Folkestone. Christmas and its festivities came and went, seeing in the New Year, leave and returning as a married man. More training, a Divisional Padres course under canvas in January, much to the amusement of the rest of the Division. This was followed by a really tough Padres Battle School in the Midlands; again much amusement from our brother officers. What's the world coming to? Padres in battle courses, what do they want with that nonsense? How often in the future months were we to be glad of having painfully learnt to crawl, dig and respect mines and booby traps. How true was the Battle School war-cry 'Dig or Die'. Every man, padres included, in 1st Army Group was to be fully trained for their particular job.

Speculation was rife at this time as to when this great event called 'The Invasion' was to take place. Amateur meteorologists talked of tides and spring equinoxes. Changes were made in the unit. A new Commanding Officer arrived, new equipment, including a car for the padre, which he was immediately told he could not take with him because of 'light scales' (regulations limiting the amount of equipment that could be taken overseas).

Finally in April another move was made under canvas, this time to beautiful surroundings near Hastings and then the work rose to a crescendo. Waterproofing of vehicles,

2

loads to be arranged, deciding what to leave and what to take on 'light scales', the excitement was getting down to the men and being reflected in the increase of questions in the Padre's Hour and the numbers at services. Even the weather began to warm up and pleasant evenings were spent on the lawn playing croquet and bowls. Memories of those evenings were to come flooding back later.

By the end of May we were all ready, but still didn't know when this great effort was to take place, and as a matter of fact, the first we actually knew about it was by being kept awake all night on June 5th by the roar of aeroplane engines overhead. It was the BBC that gave us the first news that the show was on. How soon before we joined in? We hadn't long to wait. The battalion was split into two: motor transport and marching troops. I was motor transport, my batman was marching, the car was to come on later with the residue and I began to wonder if the three of us would ever be united again.

On the evening of June 14 we left Crowhurst, driving through the night for London where we arrived in the early hours of the morning. Despite the earliness of the hour and of the fact that the campaign was just a week old, the East End was organised for our reception. As we made our way through the crowded streets, cakes, cigarettes, fruit and tea served in jam jars were thrust into the trucks by willing hands. Never had human nature shown its better side in a more fitting way.

The crusade against Nazism was on and the population, instead of beating drums and singing songs, came to give us their blessing and help. Hard fears of the blitz had wiped out the sham and hysteria, in its place was a deep sense of hope and trust in Divine Providence which could be felt.

That night as we lay on the floor of the dormitories in the transit camp the first buzz bombs arrived. At first we cheered as we heard the roar of an engine suddenly cut out – Well done the anti-aircraft boys, we said. After about the fifth one however, we began to wonder, surely even the anti-aircraft couldn't be as good as that? Next morning we discovered for the first time Hitler's new weapon. The following night we didn't lie in bed and cheer, we made for shelter.

Saturday afternoon in June – cricket or tennis perhaps. It's a lovely day, the loud speakers in the camp suddenly come to life, orders are given and we are off again. All the vehicles had to be loaded, and off we went in London buses to that hive of industry, London's Dockland. In an hour we had embarked on the *Wm. G. James*, an American Liberty ship with an American crew, a symbol of the united nations. It was a beautiful evening for a cruise. We drifted lazily down the Thames, leaving London behind and watching Hitler's latest atrocity going past us to fall – where? Some of the boys were Londoners and they peered anxiously from the stern of the boat. A great feeling of helplessness came over us all. We were soldiers; and at sea, soldiers take second place. We were in the hands of our American allies, who manned the ship. This feeling of helplessness brought men to the simple service held on Sunday morning, as we lay at anchor off Southend. All denominations joined in a short service conducted by the Divisional Senior Chaplain and myself, one a C of E and the other a Methodist. Denominational differences were forgotten as the men knelt on the deck at the communion service, compo boxes covered with a blanket making the table, but all felt His presence. Was this an omen for the future?

On Monday evening the convoy sailed, only to be held up at the other side by the weather. For a week we were cooped up in the confined space of an overcrowded ship within sight of our goal and unable to land. It was an unforgettable sight. All around us were ships of all sizes and shapes, from HMS *Renown* to motor torpedo boats. That week taught us what naval supremacy meant. There we were for six days and nights, lying helplessly off the French coast, and never once did an enemy ship dare to come anywhere near their gigantic target. True the Luftwaffe were a little more daring, but only at night, and even then ONLY ONE SHIP was hit. We were learning how superior we really were at sea and in the air – what about land?

On Saturday things began to happen. LTCs (landing craft) came alongside, winches were busy, willing hands pulled on ropes and the vehicles began to be unloaded. No docks, no harbour, straight from the hold of the Liberty ship to the deck of the LCTs, yet not one vehicle was damaged.

Eventually our turn came. The doctors' two vehicles were unloaded and off we went, under the care of the Navy, for the shore. We were able to run almost onto the beach and the trucks only had a few yards of shallow water to negotiate and we were on land again. France at last.

There was no stopping on the beaches however, we must keep going and away we went, through the small town. The civilians seemed awed and subdued. We stopped eventually to remove the waterproofing from the engine, then away again, following our own divisional signs. Many times in the future were we to realize the magnificent work done by the Red Caps, but this was our first experience.

On we went blinded and choked by the dust of the French lanes. No one who was in Normandy that summer

Beach at Arromanche where the British troops landed.

of 1944 will forget the dust; it was everywhere. A sentence from Eothen, modified, describes it – 'Dust, dust, dust, dust again, more dust'. Eventually we were met by the advance party and escorted to an orchard, and there sure enough were the marching troops waiting for us. Transport rolled in all day and by the evening we were a unit ready for action.

Chapter Two

The following day we set off for the concentration area which was a small village called Roqueville. It was only a short march of about 7 or 8 miles, but the heat, dust and French cider from excited villagers took hold of the men and the doctor was a very busy man when we arrived at the other end, dealing with bad feet and heat exhaustion. We were camped in a field and when we had settled down the Commanding Officer prepared to address the men and tell them about the future operations. It was a beautiful Sunday evening. The Commanding Officer's talk was to be at 9 o'clock and I was allowed to have my service when he was finished. All the men stayed and worshipped in the quietness of that French orchard with no outside aids to worship at all. After the service we had a celebration of holy communion and again many men, feeling God to be near, shared in the simple service in the open air. It was our first Sunday and for some, their last communion.

Next morning reconnaissance parties went forward to prepare what was to be 'a take over in the line', and that night the rest of the battalion went forward. What yesterday was dust, today was mud. The vehicles groaned forward up to the axles in mud. Our destination was the village of Cheux. I was in the rear of the column and next morning found the transport all halted and pulled off the road, some two miles or more from the battalion. Corporal Philips, my batman, Private Christian and myself tried to get the doctor's 15 cwt. vehicle through the mud lane that had been

7

Road at Cheux down which Panther tanks came and knocked out DCLI Anti-Tank Troop killing Commanding Officer.

Panther tank destroyed at Cheux.

cleared through a minefield, but two or three skids almost over the white tapes decided the issue, and Christian and I set off to walk. We eventually discovered some of the battalion who told us they had been attacked by tanks and didn't quite know what the position was further forward. Having seen our Brigade sign about 500 yards down the road we decided to call there for information. Just as we arrived an enemy plane appeared, chasing one of our artillery spotters and we all bolted to earth like rabbits. The Brigadier took me to the battalion himself and we found the doctor working in a sunken road with only his monkey box (a small box of essential medical equipment), few supplies and casualties coming in in a steady flow. As we helped where we could, we gradually heard the story of a counter attack by six tanks just as the battalion was moving into position. The air was thick with rumours but we were too busy to listen. As the day went on we eventually got the story. Six tanks had been destroyed, two by individual action with projectile infantry anti-tanks manned by Capt. Blackwall and Sgt. Hicks, the others with our own anti-tank guns. Our Commanding Officer had been killed whilst helping to man one of the guns, when most of the crew had been killed or wounded. The troop of 17 pounder anti-tank guns had been shot up before they were unlimbered and were still burning alongside the destroyed tanks. That night we had our first experience of collecting the dead, and feeling very sick, Medical Sergeant Roy Holding and I went round to collect the bodies and prepare graves. Everywhere was the stench of death. This, then, was war. A few hours before we were a raw battalion, now we were experienced troops.

The little village of Cheux was in ruins, the church was shattered, and in a corner of what remained of the church yard we prepared our first British grave and buried our comrades including our Commanding Officer. The battalion was reorganized under the second in command and HQs were set up in the same sunken lane where the doctor was working. Such was our ignorance in those days that we had the Humber brake in the gully. When we started to dig in we found the sides of the gully were solid rock. We remained nearly a week and when we left, we were still not properly dug in.

We had further casualties from intermittent mortaring and lost yet another officer. The average life of an officer during those early days was one week, and already we had lost two killed and two wounded in two days. We found ourselves in the centre of a major action and officers kept arriving from all kinds of other units in the vicinity for reports with information. They were all greeted by our mess corporal, in short sleeves and minus tin hat, with a cup of tea. Indeed Cpl. Northcott's tea was to become a legend. The hotter the action the warmer the tea. It was at Cheux that I first saw what in this war we called 'Battle Exhaustion' and perhaps this was the worst of all our casualties. Wounds can be healed and to a Christian, death has glorious possibilities, but to see men known to you personally, completely broken mentally, is a never to be forgotten experience. Perhaps the doctors can explain it, but it seemed strange that it was the apparently tough boys who went under. Our very first case was one of the battalion boxers, a young corporal who seemed as hard as nails, and yet it certainly wasn't cowardice, and a lot of silly and unkind things were said about these cases. If the authors had visited a regimental aid post and seen some of these boys, they would have changed their opinions.

On the night of June 30 we moved and there was great rejoicing to think that we were getting away from this village of death and destruction. It was only a short move to a tiny village called Colleville, two or three houses on a cross road. We were there ten days and were mortared pretty well every day. These ten days are a story in themselves.

Immediately on arrival we dug like badgers. HQ was in a little orchard, the regimental aid post was dug in in the outhouses of a chateau, and well dug in at that. Now we did almost everything in slit trenches. O. Groups (Briefing of officers) were held with officers, two to a slit. Church services were held by Companies also in slits. We ventured a communion service in one of the downstairs rooms of the chateau and later entertained the Brigadier to dinner in the same room, which had been beautifully furnished in period furnishing. The dinner was notable for the fact that we got away from tins for once, and used some of the local foods etc. which had been left behind by the vanished owners.

If ever there was a Hell Fire corner, that was it. Almost every time anyone came near, there were casualties. One night the Welsh Regiment was to pass through, and on that corner alone one Company was wiped out. Thereby hangs a tale. We were working flat out in the regimental aid post with the Welsh boys as well as our own. Incidentally as both our doctor and the medical sergeant were Welsh everyone was happy. I ran out of cigarettes for the wounded and went to my slit trench just outside for some more at about 4 a.m. When I returned after what I thought was five minutes, I found the regimental aid post deserted, not a sign of life about; until looking in the next barn, I found the Welsh Regiment regimental aid post set up with their own doctor. My five minutes had been an hour – I had gone off to sleep on my feet – and the Welsh medical officer had got through and relieved our sadly overworked staff.

Another story from the same evening. A Welsh boy was brought in with a wound in the back. When we cut away his small pack and got to him, there was nothing but a slight bruise. The shrapnel was twisted in his mess tin. He jumped up and went off guarding that pack and twisted mess tin as if they were gold.

I had an unexpected bath at Colleville. The Engineers set up their water point in our courtyard and had a big canvas tank in the centre, full of water. One bright afternoon I was washing my feet in a bowl of water in the doorway of the regimental aid post when suddenly a mortar bomb landed in this water tank and I had a free shower bath; despite the number of people about at the time, there wasn't a casualty.

We next occupied a little village near to Carpiquet aerodrome. Here we had a nasty fright. The doctor had set up shop in some outbuildings which we had carefully reinforced. He and I were sharing a loose box and during the night we were awakened by the arrival of some casualties. The doctor stumbled over something in the dark and when a light appeared, we found an unexploded German mortar bomb on the floor. It had found its way through the one small crack we had left. We gave a quiet vote of thanks to some unknown slave worker for yet one more 'dud'.

Chapter Three

On July 11 we were given orders to attack a feature called Hill 112 and after the orders had been given, David, our Intelligence officer, came to me and said, 'This will be a tough one, Padre.' How tough we fortunately did not know, and away we went at about 4 o'clock in the afternoon. We had to wait for a while in a small farmhouse about a quarter of a mile from the bottom of the hill. The doctor went forward with the medical sergeant and I was to bring the rest along. We set off with one 15 cwt. driven by Cpl. Philips with Christian and Cpl. Morgan in the back, then came the despatch rider followed by the ambulance. As we started to climb the track up the side of the hill, down came the mortars, right, left, in front, behind. Philips gritted his teeth and carried on over that 150 yards or so of open country to where the doctor was waiting in the shelter of the hedge. When we arrived and started digging we discovered the despatch rider was missing and the next news we had of him was a letter from a hospital in England.

By now it was dark, casualties were pouring in and it was impossible to work under the conditions – no light and no cover. The doctor decided to move down to the little house previously occupied and asked me to find the Adjutant and inform him. Libey, a carrier driver, offered to take me in his carrier and off we went, over another stretch of open country and delivered the message. On the way back we had to stop to let two tanks go by. This seemed strange as it was now pitch dark. It was not until the first one had passed that we realised they were German. We didn't wait after that, but shot through the gap between the first and second and arrived back at the regimental aid post rather out of breath. Casualties continued to pour in all night, together with stories of what was happening. Next morning I went up to see the Adjutant again and found him very tired, but very cool and calm reorganising what was left of the battalion. He told me the Commanding Officer had been killed, plus a number of other officers and men and asked me to go and see what I could do. So off we went in the carrier. We left the carrier in the shelter of a hedge and walked into the road to find the officer in charge. He told me where there were some bodies but on the way we found some wounded and decided to get them away whilst the carrier driver remained in the truck with the wounded whilst I brought in, or so I thought, the carrier a bit nearer. When we came to get them in however, the driver said 'This isn't my carrier sir, this one was abandoned last night, it won't go,' At the same time the Company Commander arrived and said 'Get . . . out of here, there are two German tanks just coming round the bend'. We pressed the starter of the 'abandoned carrier' and it brought us back. We never entered that wood again until months later, after the tide of battle had flowed, when we sent representatives to check up the graves of 80 officers and men and to fix a board on which was inscribed 'Cornwall Hill'.

We were now holding the side of the hill and on my visit the following morning I was sitting in a trench with David and John Fry where the doctor had remained to get at a scalp wound, much to John's disgust, when an arm appeared over the side holding out a mug of tea, followed a few minutes afterwards by a slice of bread and jam.

Memorial on Hill 112 (Cornwall Hill) Esquay.

Hill 112. General impression showing one British grave.

15

Corporal Northcott was there again. Shortly afterwards the mail arrived, such was the marvellous work done by the non-fighting part of the unit. Mail, food and ammunition arrived daily. After three days on this hill we were at last relieved and pulled out to reorganize. Unfortunately the area chosen was a gun area and that night of all nights for the first and last time, we were attacked from the air. The language used by the men was certainly not intended for the padre to hear.

Next the remnants of the battalion gathered together and we met our new Commanding Officer and Second in Command, and other new reinforcements who were arriving. Brigadier Essame came over and had dinner with us again, but some familiar faces were missing. The losses had been very heavy and our hearts were heavy also. The next day was Sunday and we split the unit into two and had our services in the open. Many men remained to take communion for the first time, and as I talked to the men during the day they all said the same thing in different words – their sense of helplessness was forcing them back to God. Here is the secret of true religion. It is when we lose all our artificial 'props' that we realise that Christianity is not an extra or a luxury but the one thing we cannot live without. Those men were learning to live without all the things they had previously regarded as essentials: home, sleep, food, sport, entertainments, but they could not do without God and they admitted it.

After our brief refit we returned to the Hill again and spent another week in this most unpleasant spot. We had casualties almost every day. Fortunately the German is a very methodical creature and we learnt there were times each day when it was safe to move around and other times when it was not, and we profited from this knowledge. During this week my car arrived and so we were complete again. The car was quickly in use as an extra ambulance, the little Austin Ten being able to take two stretcher cases with a little adaptation.

At last we were relieved and came out of the line altogether for the first time. For three days we were miles away from danger. I was ordered to report back to Army HQ where the Deputy Chaplain General had established his HQ, and where the Divisional Padres had three days rest. There was work to be done, however, of a different but still difficult kind. We had an opportunity to catch up on our correspondence. To write to the relatives of men who have been killed in action is not an easy job, but it was one that had to be done by the padre. During the campaign I wrote over 300 letters with respect to fatal casualties alone. Two-thirds of the recipients replied, generally wanting further particulars, but the most encouraging thing of all was the tone of those letters. They are my most treasured possessions. The bravery and Christian faith displayed in that file is truly amazing. Only one of those letters is in any way bitter in tone. Here again in time of great sorrow the fundamental things are revealed, and the simple message of the Christian hope of eternal life brought strength to those who were left to mourn. This part of our duty was really worthwhile and often in later days when I felt depressed, I would read some of the letters in my files and my strength was renewed.

Chapter Four

After our three day break we were quickly on the move again and within 24 hours we had another job near the village of Jurges. The regimental aid post was established just behind the village whilst the battalion were to capture another hill feature which became known as Tiger Hill. Casualties kept coming in, each with a different story and the air was full of rumours about this and that Company. It was strange how the facts became distorted when men were wounded.

After working hard all day we tried to snatch some sleep and were very annoyed when the area was shelled. Next morning however we were able to move forward again and discovered the real facts. The greatest difficulty was to recover our dead in this very thick undergrowth. It took me 28 hours to find and bury 16 men. The following day we were able to clear the rubble from one room of a house and hold a service. We no longer waited until Sunday for church services but fitted them in as and when we could.

August Bank Holiday with perfect holiday weather and a pleasant piece of country in which to spend the day. Life seemed more or less uneventful. The Carrier platoon was out doing a small job of work but that was all. Most of the remainder of the battalion were lying back and enjoying the sun. About tea time the Brigadier arrived and we knew something was 'on'. It was one of those things which happen so often in war, a quick change of plan and we had to set off immediately. That night we went over the top of

Mount Pincon and made a surprise attack on the village of Plessis Grimault, a brilliant piece of strategy which brought us into the village with hardly a casualty despite the fact that it was strongly held. We took a big bag of prisoners that night including an officer who amazed the Commanding Officer by giving him a Nazi salute.

As often happened, getting into the village was one thing, staying in it was another very different thing. We had to put up with a good deal of mortaring and a direct hit on part of Battalion Headquarters killed some of our prisoners as well as our own men. But even then our casualties were still light. The greatest problem we had was due to the fact that we had entered the village by the back entrance, so to speak, and one or two people who tried to reach us and one or two of our own men who went back with messages, just vanished as a result of taking the wrong road. Fortunately they were taken prisoner and most of them eventually trickled through to us, but it made most of us very wary as to which way we went.

The war now had become one of movement and we were brought back to the small village of Clemensil to reorganize and then back to work again at a place called Le Quesnes. At this time no one quite knew where the Germans were and in this village we found our gunners in front of us, yet we picked up one or two German stragglers before being switched over yet again to capture the village of La Tralodier. At this time the strain of loss of sleep and mental tension began to be felt. Fortunately we had a respite and to quote an example, one officer slept for 48 hours without a break.

Our next objective was to cross the river Noireau and capture the ridge of high ground known as Berjou Ridge

Le Plessis Grimault. First German Tiger Tank to be destroyed.

Blown bridge over River Noireau with minefield in foreground.

and the other side. On the way up to the river the regimental aid post was established in a small house in a deserted village. One old lady was left with her husband, who had died from shock caused by the fighting. It was impossible to get in touch with any civil authorities at this time and so I had the unpleasant task of burying him, temporarily, in his own front garden.

Next morning we moved on, leaving the widow alone until our message back to the civil authorities brought her relief. This instance is one of the many similar untold incidents and side issues of modern war. The attack went in next morning and after hard fighting was completely successful, by the evening we were on top of the ridge and after dinner I went fishing in the river with the Brigadier in surroundings that were a delight to the eye and seemed far remote from war. As a matter of fact, although we had been fighting all that day, by next morning we were over 100 miles from the nearest Germans and had our backs to them. We had cleaned up one of the pockets in the Falaise Gap and were now miles behind the line.

The following day was Thursday and we had a service in the open. We didn't wait for Sundays any more. As a matter of fact we were still there on Sunday so had another service and the attendances on both occasions were good, particularly at the first one which was a memorial service for the sixteen men who had been killed and were buried in the orchard nearby. We remained here long enough to get cleaned up properly for once and the weather was very kind to us so that living in the open was no hardship (rather the reverse). We enjoyed a brief holiday and were all in good spirits.

On August 23 we were on the move again, but this time

it was a long move. By the evening we had reached the small town of Gase and for the first time saw French civilians in something like normal surroundings. We spent the night here and had an interesting 24 hours. The Signal officer was a brilliant French linguist and he arranged for us to have our evening meal at a local café. This was a complete and welcome change and incidentally gave the mess staff a rest. We had a magnificent dinner in comfortable surroundings, still a long way from any disturbances. Unfortunately for me, my car had developed valve trouble and as we were to move on next day my batman and myself and a fitter were up most of the night to get it ready, and we didn't move next morning. However, such is life.

It was here that we saw for the first time, collaborators being paraded through the streets with shorn heads, and it was a most unpleasant sight too. A woman minus hair even though otherwise well-dressed, is not a nice sight and this side of the underground movement was received with mixed feelings by the troops. We were quickly on the move again and passed through part of the American sector through places of which we had heard on the radio, Argenton and other equally destroyed towns and villages, until eventually we reached the Seine at Vernon and so began yet another chapter.

Chapter Five

We arrived in the outskirts of Vernon on a perfect August afternoon at about 4 o'clock and pulled the trucks off the road under a beautiful avenue of trees. We had a long wait whilst the Commanding Officer went off for orders and some of us sat in a little café and talked to some of the civilians. The town had been liberated two or three days previously but the Germans were at the other side of the river. The local inhabitants were quite unconcerned, however, and were taking their Saturday afternoon strolls all dressed up as if it were peace time. It was a strange mixture of war and peace at this stage of the campaign and we found it difficult to reconcile the two. The French civilians no longer fled, they knew that most of the actions lasted only a matter of hours and so took what shelter they could and reappeared from all over the place immediately the shooting stopped.

We discovered that our job was to widen the bridgehead already made by another brigade, to allow the armour to cross, and then we went in the late evening, on towards the village of Presagny. We made our headquarters in an orphanage presided over by a bearded lay brother. After a good meal we went to bed. Somehow things had gone so well generally that we were lulled into a false sense of security.

We went upstairs to sleep in a big dormitory. Our slumbers were rudely awakened to the whizz of bullets going past the windows and we awoke to find ourselves in the middle of a battle. The country hereabouts was thickly wooded and a party of Germans had infiltrated through our forward positions. The regimental aid post was in the centre of the defence position. The attack was beaten off with great help from the artillery, who dropped shells all around us without touching any of our own men. You can never be sure of anything in war and this was one of the occasions which proved it. But as always, morning came and with it, we hoped, the tanks. The Germans however thought otherwise and one salvo from their guns destroyed the bridge built by the Sappers and a fresh start had to be made. We also discovered the bearded gentleman was a suspect and he had to be taken back to Vernon for interrogation. As he was in some measure connected with the church the padre was asked to take him back in his truck – another strange job to be done.

The next day the bridgehead was further widened by an attack we made on the village of Panilleuse. This went very well with few casualties and by evening we were being feted by the inhabitants as liberators. This was our final real experience of liberating a populated village and the gratitude and stories we heard made us all feel that after all, this was a job worth doing.

By now the bridge was open and armour streaming across. For three weeks we remained here and watched the whole might of the British 2nd Army and the Tactical Air Force go past, It was a most impressive and encouraging sight as well as giving us the opportunity for a real rest.

There was a certain amount of work to be done in the way or reorganization. We received a lot of reinforcements who had to be absorbed into what by now was in every sense a team. But we also had some relaxation. ENSA on this occasion did us well. We had a big show in the open air with a portable stage mounted on a lorry at which Flanagan and Allen, Kay Cavendish, and Florence Desmond appeared on their way through to Brussels. The Germans had left behind in Panilleuse a fair-sized barrack room which incidentally they had built next door to the church. This room became in turn theatre, cinema, and church as well as providing a billet for some of the men, and on one remarkable occasion became a dance hall, despite its stone floor.

There were not many girls in the village and so on the evening of the dance I was sent in my truck to the next village to find some more. This was accomplished by the simple process of going to the first farm in the village and asking the girls there to come. They immediately ran round the village and collected the others and the truck returned loaded with partners. At the end of the dance they were all prepared to walk the two miles back with their new found escorts and the padre wasn't at all popular when he took them all back again in the truck. The band on this occasion was rather unique. The pianist was the Intelligence officer, a Captain, also Organ Scholar at Cambridge. The saxophonist was a Major, one of the Company Commanders; the drums were manned by the Second in Command of the battalion, also of course a Major. The Signal sergeant was the fourth member and a private soldier completed the ensemble. It was a good band too.

We also discovered that Paris was only 70 miles away and eventually it was arranged for us to take parties of the men in for a day at a time. We set off in the early morning and arrived in Paris about 9.30 to 10 a.m. and were immediately besieged. We were almost the first and only British troops in the area. We were welcomed with open arms. Paris was a different place from what some of us knew and amid all the rejoicing and outward smartness of appearance, we could feel something of the pain and hardship suffered for so long. It was however an experience not to be missed – Paris in the early days of the liberation. Of course we bought perfume and other presents for home. We hadn't spent any money since leaving England and it was a new experience. It was very pleasant for many officers and men to sit in the sun in the Champs Elysées and watch Paris going by, mainly on bicycles. What in peace time was a French national sport was now a national means of transport. The famous Paris taxies had disappeared and were replaced by cycle taxies.

On the way back we called at Versailles and showed a party of the men where the last peace treaty was signed and we wondered about the next.

On September 14 we were on the move again and it was a long one. We had a motor tour through Northern France into Belgium, passing through places made famous by our fathers – Mons, Arras, Cambrai and others. All along the route were cheering crowds and convoy discipline was rather difficult to maintain as every time we stopped for whatever reason, the trucks were besieged. We crossed into Belgium without any customs formalities, and spent the night in a big school at Brain de Comte. Offers of hospitality came from almost every house, but next morning we were off again to the same accompaniment of cheering crowds. We missed Brussels but passed Waterloo and had a very pleasant ride through the woods which encircle the Belgian capital.

We stopped eventually just north of Diest and bivouacked

in the fields. We had three days here and one of them was a Sunday. Our services were held in the open and once again despite the lack of outside aids to worship, both at the communion service and the service which followed, we felt that God was with us.

We knew that a big plan was on foot and later that day we heard the name Arnhem for the first time and learnt what our job was to be in the big scheme, which, if successful, we knew might well end the war.

Author and vehicle somewhere in Europe.

Doctor and Padre with RAP staff and captured German troop carrier adapted as an armoured ambulance.

28

Chapter Six

The task of 30 Corps was to link up with the Airborne Division at various points and our own task was to provide the last link in the chain. Away we went, with the Guards and the 50 Division in front of us. We travelled day and night, passing through the 50 Division at the Albert Canal and Hochtel and so still behind the Guards into Holland, linking up as planned. This time of course we were given an even greater welcome by the Dutch as we really were liberating them and receiving all the pent up emotions of four years of occupation. We passed through Eindoven in the middle of the night and the giant Philips factory stood out in bold relief.

By now we were a long thin line with nothing at either side for protection, but we got through without incident and on the 21st September reached the outskirts of Nijmegen right behind the Guards who had first entered the town. Here we paused and watched the war in the air. Dakotas were passing overhead and dropping supplies, Spitfires and German fighters having dog fights in the clear blue sky criss-crossed with vapour trails. We heard that the Bridge was in our hands. In the evening we moved up into Nijmegen itself and discovered that next day we were to become the spearhead and must contact the 1st British Airborne Division still holding out a few miles away.

On the afternoon of the 22nd we crossed the river by the railway bridge. One of our sister battalions in the Brigade led off to capture the small village of Ousterhout on the

View of Nijmegen Rail Bridge from 'the island'.

other side whilst we sat and watched. We saw the civilians evacuate the village, then came about 200 German prisoners and the bulk of the civilians turned round and went back home. Liberation in two hours.

We now had the job of trying to make the final contact with the hard pressed Red Devils and off we went with our supporting squadron of tanks and two DUWKs, (amphibious vehicles used for assault crossing of water obstacles) loaded with supplies which we hoped to get across the river later that night.

No one who took part will forget that ride, or rather for most people, walk, to Driel. We set off at dusk and by-passed Elst which was strongly held. At one stage in the journey we discovered four enemy tanks in the column. CSM Philip and Pte. Brown of A Company with a projectile infantry anti-tank accounted for all four, firing it at very short range. Pte. Brown, although badly wounded, survived to receive a very well-earned Military Medal and CSM Philip, also wounded, received his Distinguished Service Medal.

Our leading Company reached the village in twenty minutes having covered a distance of ten miles by a roundabout route, over high dyke roads. At Valburg we had to stop the rejoicing of the inhabitants because the Germans were so near. The link up with the Polish Airborne Brigade on the south side of the river was complete but unfortunately we could not get the DUWKs across to aid men on the other side. The situation behind us was not at all clear but there we were on the banks of the Leh.

Next morning I visited a Polish Advanced Dressing Station in the village which was run by Polish doctors and two Dutch nurses, who lived in the village. The patients were Polish parachutists, British parachutists and an RAF Air Crew who had been hidden by the local people, our own wounded were arriving and morphia was very short. I went back to our own regimental aid post which was about 500 yards away, for some supplies. When I returned I found a large hole where the door had been, a shell having landed on the doorstep. Fortunately none of the patients was hurt but a nurse and a doctor and some civilians were now added to the list of casualties.

The following day the situation was sufficiently clear for us to evacuate back and ambulances began to arrive. Meantime we still had not crossed the river except for getting about fifty of the Polish force over. General Horrocks, the Corps Commander arrived and studied the situation from the top of the church tower, a most unhealthy spot. The rest of the story is history. The DUWKs

Nijmegen Road Bridge after capture by Guards Armoured.

were sent across and the following night we started to evacuate all that we could. Thus ended a glorious failure.

We remained in the vicinity for two or three days more before being finally relieved. We returned to the village of Ousterhout by way of Andelst where we made ourselves very comfortable in a jam factory, with HQ in the manager's house. We had a piano here, and David our Intelligence officer, who was a brilliant musician, entertained us in the evenings. He composed a song which described the journey to Driel which quickly became a battalion signature tune. We also paid visits to Officers and Other Ranks Clubs already established in Nijmegan. This was quite an adventure and involved crossing the Nijmegan bridge which was still under fire. Tea dances were being held at the Officers Club which was about 1000 yards from the bridge. The local civilian WVS ran the club and provided dance partners. The Other Ranks Club was equally popular, being situated in a cinema. Such is the British mentality that in the midst of battle we could provide relaxations, the moral effect of which was invaluable.

There was a Dutch Reform Church in Ousterhout and so for the first time since landing we had our services in a church.

The area between the two rivers became known as 'the Island' and was occupied by the Division. Further to the west the 101 American Airborne Division (famous later in the Ardennes) were protecting the left flank and on the day we were due to be relieved orders came to go to their help. The battle centred round Ofheusden and was, I think, the most unpleasant twelve hours of the whole campaign. Our regimental aid post was under fire all the time. By a miracle no-one was wounded despite the fact of direct hits on the farm buildings. When we pulled out at midnight, every vehicle in Battalion HQ had at least one hole in it somewhere. We were told we were to have a rest at last and although we had had a good number of casualties which were high, we crossed the river and went to a little village west of Nijmegan called Ewigh. We had one day's rest and then had to move over to the outskirts of the Reichwald Forest – such is life in wartime.

We remained in this area for a month, in and out of forward positions, moving every three or four days. A further hit on the regimental aid post temporarily established in the little post office at Mook, again saw us all escape without injury.

This sort of thing was lightened by occasional trips into Nijmegan during short spells in reserve. Nijmegan was by now equipped with cinema, clubs run by YMCA and other welfare services, all done within a month of its liberation, and with the Germans still too near to be comfortable.

Then came a new development, we were to move south for the attack on Geilenkirchen. This was welcomed by all as it meant a long ride away from any trouble and a change of surroundings.

Chapter Seven

We arrived at a little village called Merkelbeck which was just outside the mining town of Brunsum. We were now right on the German border. Our billets were in the miners' houses and as many of the men knew something about coalmining, friendships were made very quickly. We were also able to use the magnificent pit head baths which were a real luxury, plenty of hot water and a real bath. During this pause before the next action, which was to take us into Germany itself, we were able to hold Padre's Hours for the first time since coming overseas.

I was anxious to learn what effect their experiences had had on the men. I took a census by asking the question 'How many of you now believe there is something in what the church has been saying about God?' 80 per cent admitted to a change of heart in this respect. Much has been said and written about slit trench religion, but the fact remains, when all our earthly props are knocked away, then we come to know God. Here is a practical demonstration of the teaching of Christ, that it is necessary to feel a need for God before we can really experience true religion. We felt that need and it was met. Men were not spared from death or pain, but they did receive strength to carry on when their natural inclination was to give up.

Let me give one example. A boy came to me and told me he couldn't carry on any longer. His nerve had gone. I knew him rather well and asked him if he still believed in God. He said he did. I then asked him to try once more and ask

God for strength to carry him through. He came to me after the next action and said, 'It works, Sir'.

On November 18 we crossed the border into Germany for the first time. We were to capture a village and so cut off the Germans in Geilenkirchen, which was to be attacked by the Americans. The weather was atrocious, heavy rain had fallen and the cart track along which we advanced became impassable. We got through on foot and captured the village of Hocheid. The regimental aid post was established in the cellar of what remained of a house, which wasn't much. Here we carried on for two days until the transport arrived. My truck and the doctor's truck were parked in the yard of the regimental aid post and shortly after my truck received a direct hit and everything in it was destroyed. As we had no time to unload anything, we lost all we had in the way of comforts as well as personal kit. However, we considered ourselves lucky not to be inside it at the time.

We were now asked to push on through a wood to the village of Hoven. No one fancied the task and the weather was getting worse. The attack went in however, and despite heavy losses D Company eventually reached the objective, only to be counter-attacked. Ten men came back. Altogether between 12 midday and the following morning, nearly 200 men passed through the regimental aid post. This was our second heavy loss. We collected the dead and took them back to Brunsum where we had established a Divisional Cemetery. The Dutch people covered the graves with flowers and months afterwards I received word that a rose tree had been planted on every grave. There were by this time about 500 graves.

We were now relieved in order to reorganize our depleted forces and returned to a monastery near Brunsum. The monks and theological students did all they could to help us and for a month we rested and absorbed the reinforcements which were arriving to make up our losses. We got rid of our mud and filth at the pit head baths and held a memorial service in the refectory of the monastery. The Senior Chaplain of the Division came and gave the address. I had now to start and collect some more kit and a new truck. A jeep arrived on temporary loan, which was a great help.

On the night before we left to go into the line again, the monks gave us a concert which was enjoyed by all. Even though we didn't understand the words of the Dutch songs, we found one or two that we had in common. *Stille Nacht* was sung in English by the troops and in German by the monks as another example of the universality of religion to all nations. We felt bound together as we worshipped together at the close of the concert.

After a week's rest, we returned to the line, but this time in a quieter sector. After a week we came back to the little German village of Grotenrath and for a fortnight we were busy training hard. I managed to hold Padre's Hours once again in order to talk to the new men. I found them of two main types. On the one hand there were those who were keen to get on with the job and get it finished, and on the other hand some of the younger ones had not had the time or the opportunity to obtain either responsibility or a sense of duty. They adopted an attitude of toughness, not against the enemy, but against the army. Some of them became a problem later, but the large majority were keen and very soon in their carriage and bearing showed that they would be worthy of the men they were to replace.

It was at this time that we first contacted the Dutch

Resistance Movement. I was asked to organise a dance and after a visit to the Burgomaster was referred to a Dutch lady, and made for the address. This story is typical of many.

The family consisted of father, a doctor who had spent some months in a concentration camp and mother who was busy doing welfare work although an old lady. One son had spent a year in hiding in Belgium and was now actively engaged with our forces, and another was working with the Americans. The daughter of the family was at home, having forty-eight hours rest. She helped the American airborne troops to enter Vegel by acting as a guide and had been in the forefront of the fight there. She was now secretary to one of the leaders of Dutch resistance and a charming girl who spoke English, French and German perfectly. She donated the whole of the leave helping me to make the dance a success. These were typical of the people we were liberating after years of untold hardship and pain. That family had been separated for years, each playing his or her part. I was shown where the telephone was hidden which was in direct communication with the Resistance Movement.

This house now became a second home for those officers who could spare an hour or two away from the fighting and in the quietness of that home and with the help of the family we learnt to forget for a time our cares and problems. Unfortunately, though the war is now over, the price is still being paid. A letter which I received in August of this year was to inform me that the daughter had had a breakdown and was seriously ill – and knowing something of her experiences I was not surprised.

Chapter Eight

As Christmas drew near, we began to wonder how we would spend it. Would we be in or out of the line? Our doubts were soon resolved when we were told we would spend Christmas in the Dutch town of Tilburg and have a really good holiday before tackling the next big job scheduled to take place early in the New Year, whilst the frost made the roads hard. I went off to Tilburg with the advance party to arrange our services and entertainment, but as often in war the best laid plans of even the highest authorities, are upset. Von Runsted launched an offensive in the Ardennes and the battalion never reached Tilburg. The column was actually on the road when the orders came to halt. Billets had to be found quickly without the normal advance party, still in Tilburg and eventually the battalion was housed in the Belgian village of Bilsen. We were at one hour's notice to move, which made it rather difficult to arrange anything.

On Christmas morning we held a well-attended communion service, followed by the morning service, at which about 500 men were present. Both these services were held on the top floor of a factory, the men sitting on the floor, packing cases making the communion table. After the service came the Christmas dinner and despite all difficulties, we were able to give the men a real dinner of turkey, Christmas puddings and all the usual adjuncts to the Christmas festivities. The officers as usual spent the day with the men, waiting on them at dinner. On Boxing Day we had our own celebrations, until at 10 o'clock in the evening we received orders to move early next morning. Of all the times to choose to move a battalion, this was just about the worst.

Nevertheless in the early hours of the morning we said goodbye to our Belgian hosts, who had helped us to have the greatest of family festivals in their homes, and set off again. The weather was seasonable enough, but instead of a fine day we had to brave the cold in the trucks. We arrived in Holland once more having crossed the Maas again and were billeted in the village of Elslo. We had a very pleasant fortnight here. Although there was lots of snow and the temperature was below zero most days we did a great deal of training, but also managed some recreation. Although the village was small, there was a café with a small stage and a wooden floor. This became in turn church, cinema, theatre and dance hall. The village also boasted a dance band who performed nobly whilst the troops taught the Dutch girls the Lambeth Walk and other English eccentricities. This sort of life was far too good to last of course, and on the coldest morning of the year we had to move. It was so cold that the anti-freeze mixture in the vehicles didn't help and the transport officer had more than one problem to face.

As always, we all arrived at our destination eventually, and what a destination. We were back in the Geilenkirchen area, living in trenches and cellars in the middle of winter. The next fortnight was probably the most uncomfortable period of our lives, just sitting in the cold, about 1000 yards, in some places much less, away from the enemy.

Five things remain in my memory of this fortnight. The first was a communion service held in a cellar in the ruined village of Rischden at which 95 men gathered together and knelt in the straw to worship. Truly God was in that place.

Most of these men were our special team who were experts in patrolling into the enemy positions at night. They felt their need of God. Another incident concerned an RAF Typhoon pilot. He was shot down over the German lines and dislocated his shoulder blade. He wrapped his parachute round him and hid in the snow for two days. On the third day, to use his own words 'I was a bit cold and decided to go home'. He walked about four miles and startled one of our sentries by walking in over ground where mines were as numerous as daisies in a meadow. The Squadron leader was startled himself when he was shown the size of the minefield he had so calmly walked through and survived.

During this period I had some interesting talks with men in holes in the ground, where we huddled together to keep warm. These talks taught me more about the strength of character of the working people of Britain than years of social study had done. Seen under these conditions these boys were the salt of the earth; rough, uncultured many of them, yet their cheerfulness and courage were of the highest. After six months of hard fighting under difficult conditions, there was still a great sense of fellowship born of our sharing these difficulties with each other.

Here is another lesson one can learn from war. To really create a Christian fellowship, all the members must share the experiences of the others. A parson cannot preach to people whose way of life he does not understand, and before the war it was unfortunately true that one half of the world did not know how the other half lived. In those few months we were beginning to learn each other's problems and difficulties, strengths and weaknesses. The experience gained in these days will, I hope, sow the seeds of future mutual understanding and co-operation.

Chapter Nine

At the end of January came a fresh move. This time even greater secrecy than usual surrounded our movements, but there was no danger of careless talk at this time; we had a new topic of conversation, leave. We rejoiced or commiserated with each other according to the luck we had had in the draw. The first batch had already gone, having been kitted out with new suits, collars, ties, etc. for the occasion. I was lucky and left the battalion at the beginning of February for that precious seven days at home.

The arrangements were magnificent. We assembled at Bourg Leopold, boarded the train, not the comfortable sort we had at home, but it went and in the right direction. We left at 6 o'clock at night and arrived in Calais at 7 the next morning – a much battered Calais but who cared? Breakfast documentation and then a rest until called for the boat. There was a walk of about a mile from the Transit Camp to the ship, and I can still see the six foot-odd Scots Lieutenant Colonel striding down the road carrying a child's tricycle in one hand. The boys behind loved it.

It seemed strange to be back in England again but I'm afraid the joy of being at home was marred by the things one saw and heard. True we were cheered as our special train passed the stations, but we found that selfishness and bad manners were everywhere in evidence. We who had learnt through our hardships to live together were hurt and dismayed by this attitude everywhere present at home. I am writing these words from India and the newspapers are full of strikes and disputes even now, when the war is finished. Did our comrades die in vain? Is this the better world for which we fought? We who served together implore you to learn our secret of self-forgetfulness for the common cause.

It was strange also to sit and read about actions you had heard planned and knew that your comrades were engaged in. I felt a certain sense of guilt at not being with them. The seven days soon passed and back we went to rejoin the battalion, feeling at least fitter for the rest. I had slept most of the seven days.

I caught up with the battalion in what was left of the historic town of Cleve, which wasn't very much. We were now seeing for the first time the total devastation that was coming to Germany. Hardly a building remained whole in the whole of the town. Truly this was the 'abomination of desolation' and worse was to follow. The battle of the Reichwald was still in progress although I had missed the initial stages.

We advanced in the Goch, Colcar and Xanten area and began to meet German civilians. In November they had retreated with the army, now they remained behind in the midst of their shattered homes, eking out an existence and beginning to feel disillusion. They were servile and obedient, giving no trouble at all. We also saw evidence of the systematic looting of Europe. We now lived in German houses and in them all, whether it was a small cottage or a schloss, we found articles from all over Europe.

We had further complications now of civilian wounded, the people stayed in their homes whilst a battle raged in the streets and inevitably some were hurt. Civil administration had broken down and we found ourselves having to evacuate civilians and troops of both sides, often in the same ambulance. We were also faced with violent contrasts. We had German brutality in evidence in cunning booby traps and methods of fighting on one hand, and signs of culture and breeding all around us in the houses on the other, where works of the great composers rested on the grand piano just as they had been left. The classics were all on the bookshelves, often in the original tongue. The furniture and architecture were good. And so we asked ourselves, which is the real Germany? We are still trying to find the answer.

Chapter Ten

We were moved back to the area of Gennap in Holland to prepare for the next action, which we hoped would be the final one. We had to leave very early in the morning and then were parked for a few hours on the roadside. David sat in my truck and read Keats to me; our thoughts and conversation were far removed from our surroundings. We had learnt another secret – that it is possible to overcome even the worst environment if you do but try.

Our home for the next two weeks was in a shattered village, but we managed to make it habitable. The weather was very good and we saw nature triumph over the desolation. Crocuses and daffodils appeared in the gardens of the shattered houses. My batman had flowers on my table every day for a fortnight. Our services were held in a barn and in the open and amidst the great amount of training to be done, we managed to hold our Padre's Hours. The men at this time were beginning to sense the end of the fighting and by common consent the discussions began to centre round the future; the kind of world we wanted and how we were to get it. We talked about the problem of the link between our army life and our home life. Many of us had had our first real contact with the Church through war padres and it was my task to convince the men that the same fellowship would be possible at their own local church. I hope that now the men are returning this is being done. If the right approach of friendliness and understanding coupled with a real interest in the men as men and not as 'prospective customers' (to use a phrase one of them used in a criticism of the Church) then we can expect great things. It is fatal to create the impression, however unintentionally, that we want them to fill empty pews.

On the evening of 26 March we crossed the Rhine, our last great obstacle. It was a beautiful moonlit night and we had no trouble until we reached the other side and began to push out. We were now fighting desperate men and the fury of despair drove the Germans to every trick that they could find; shells, mortars, mines and booby traps of all kinds were encountered and still we pushed on.

The geography of this part of Europe is interesting. We crossed the Rhine near Rees into Germany and then as we pushed on we were soon in Holland again with the usual cheering crowds and happy faces. Easter weekend was spent on the move, but on the following Friday we stayed for a few hours in the Dutch town of Oldenzaal where I discovered a magnificent Dutch Reform Church. It was built in 1935 and is a fine example of modern church architecture, designed in brick and furnished in unpolished oak. By courtesy of the pastor we were able to have our Easter service and communion. The church was full and I felt the great joy of once again ministering to my men in a building that really helped our worship.

Next day we moved on but the memory of that service remained. We re-entered Germany and found a notice on the border 'You are now entering Germany, Behave like conquerors. No Fraternisation'. We halted for the night at the next town and two of the officers went into a big house in order to obtain accommodation. They marched across the parquet floor like conquerors, to be greeted by a lady who asked in perfect English 'What can I do for you?' The first civilian we had conquered was an English girl! She had a little boy of six or seven who also spoke English and who spent the rest of the day eagerly talking to the troops in the house. His mother told us something of her story, which was later verified. She had married a German in 1937 and he being pro-British had been moved to Austria. His wife had to remain behind and suffer at the hands of the local Nazis.

We passed on next day after sending the particulars back to the military government officials. The fighting became a series of delaying actions and many casualties were caused as the result of mines. At this stage every life lost was due to the senseless prolongation of destruction carried out by the German High Command. Despite the delays we pressed on; the engineers removed road blocks and made diversions and on we went. We were moving so quickly now that rather amusing situations developed. Here is one of them.

We entered one village in the middle of the night and established the regimental aid post in what appeared to be an empty house. Next morning the owners reappeared and were allowed to remain next door. We in the meantime searched the area and discovered a young German NCO hiding in a wood about 100 yards away. He was brought to the regimental aid post to be questioned, and met his wife! He was trying to reach home and had hidden the previous night intending to surprise his wife next morning. we arrived first however, and instead of remaining at home, as a pseudo civilian, he went back as a prisoner of war after a tearful scene on the doorstep. As a matter of fact his wife

47

was lucky she knew where her husband was, and that he was safe. The majority of the women knew nothing at all about their men. Postal and transfer services had been dislocated for months.

We passed on through Cloppenburg which was nothing but a mass of ruins and in a village not far from the town we halted again. Here we met our final genuine unashamed Nazi woman who even at this stage in April 1945 firmly believed that Hitler by some miracle would still win the war. She had blind unquestioning faith in the regime, even with British troops occupying her house. This was the sort of mentality with which we were faced.

We were now converging on Bremen and were rather excited at the prospect of helping to capture such a big prize. We crossed the autobahn running between Bremen and Hamburg and then swung round in order to enter the town from the north-east. We arrived in the suburb of Osterholz on April 26th and spent the night in the trim little suburban houses. We were about six miles outside the city but even here there was a good deal of damage. The house in which we established the regimental aid post belonged to one of the Bremen Police Force, and the first thing they said to us was 'Thank God you have come. Now there will be no more air raids.' These people were totally broken by the terrific onslaught of the RAF.

Next morning we entered the city proper in order to help with the mopping up and to control the slave workers. These latter were a grave problem, they numbered about 20,000 and had broken loose in the city, obtained large stocks of alcohol, of which there was an abundant supply, and also weapons. Drunken men and women, well-armed, find it hard to distinguish between friend and foe and we had the difficult task of restoring order and curbing the exuberance of men released from slavery.

That night we had a guard on the civilian prison and a German Naval Establishment, full of WRNS. We were occupying a position in the west end of the city in the large houses of the wealthy merchants; or what was left of them. Here again we saw another side of the German mentality. These people complained because we were in their houses, they didn't see why they should be inconvenienced and forced to live in one room for a time. This may sound fantastic but it is actual fact, they genuinely felt they were being imposed upon. So much was this in evidence, that the Commanding Officer called them together and informed them that they, as intelligent and responsible Germans, were the real people responsible for supporting the regime. It was interesting to study their expressions. The women wept, the men were sullen, but the younger members of the families were unmoved.

We were busier in the regimental aid post with civilian casualties than anything else, as a matter of fact this great city was taken very cheaply, only the SS, who had dug themselves in in the Burgher Park, gave any trouble, and then not for long.

We moved back to Osterholz the following day and prepared to clear up the odd pockets of resistance in the Cuxhaven peninsular. As I talked to the men that night, two topics of conversation were dominant. The first was the destruction of Bremen. We all felt the same; such destruction could not but make us wonder what man would do next. A whole city lay in ruins and not one building remained whole in that vast area. The second question followed from the first. How long would this senseless destruction go on? Even at this stage, small groups of Germans were fighting desperately and inflicting casualties which made us feel rather bitter against their apparently deliberate attempt to destroy as many of us as they could in their own destruction.

We were to have one more interesting experience before the finish of the campaign. We knew there was a big POW camp in the vicinity and were just beaten in the race to liberate it. We were on the spot immediately afterwards however, and the sight of thousands of men wild with joy, riding on anything they could find, or just walking along the road, free to move for the first time in five years, was a marvellous experience. It was a Merchant Navy Camp and had been run by the German Navy, which meant that conditions were rather better than the average. There seems to be a certain fellowship amongst sailors that even war does not entirely eradicate.

We were now in the remains of a village called Badenstedt in rather miserable surroundings, as all the houses were damaged and the place was already over-crowded with refugees. We made the most of it however and in the evening of May 4th we entertained some of the released prisoners. In the middle of dinner the news of the cease-fire arrived. The rest of the evening was a riotous outburst of joy. Everything that could be fired, from Very lights to the 6 pounder anti-tank guns, was fired. The civilians were frightened to death but that night no one was interested in Germans. Men wept and laughed alternately and it was well on into the morning before we could settle down for some sleep.

The war was over at last, for us at least. On Sunday May 6 we held our Thanksgiving Services. It was impossible to get all the men together so we split the battalion into three and we finished our active service worship as we had started, in a barn. Once again we had no aids to worship, but on this day of all days, none was needed.

Epilogue

The battalion moved on to the banks of the river Elbe where we settled down in pleasant surroundings to the task of reorganising the country. The fighting was over but the hardest work remained. How that work succeeds remains to be seen. We can but pray that the victory obtained by the sacrifice and suffering of our youth will not be turned to defeat by those who make the peace. We who fought present to you our trophy – a shattered but not destroyed world. May we together work and live that by God's help it may be restored.